Arlington
NATIONAL CEMETERY

EDGAR
EARL
WEMPLE
NEW YORK
PVT
STU ARMY
TNG CORPS
WORLD WAR I
OCT 31 1896
DEC 10 1955

BY BOB TEMPLE

Published by The Child's World®
1980 Lookout Drive • Mankato, MN 56003-1705
800-599-READ • www.childsworld.com

Acknowledgments
The Child's World®: Mary Berendes, Publishing Director
The Design Lab: Design
Jody Jensen Shaffer: Editing
Red Line Editorial: Photo Research

Photo credits
Shutterstock Images, cover, 6, 10; Carol M. Highsmith/Library of
Congress, 5, 13, 17; Alexander Gardner/Library of Congress,
9; An Van de Wal/Shutterstock Images, 14; Michael Reynolds/
EPA/Corbis, 18; Zack Frank/Shutterstock Images, 21

ISBN 9781623239534
LCCN 2013947297

Printed in the United States of America
Mankato, MN
November, 2013
PA02189

ABOUT THE AUTHOR

Bob Temple is an author and award-winning journalist who has enjoyed a career in newspapers and online journalism. He is also the president of an editorial services and Web content firm based in the Minneapolis-St. Paul area. Bob and his wife, Teri, are the parents of three children. He enjoys traveling and playing golf.

TABLE OF CONTENTS

★ ★ ★

Fighting for Freedom

★ ★ ★

America is a great place to live. Americans are free to choose where they live, where they work, what they own, how they worship, and more. Our many freedoms are a big part of what makes America such a great place. Over the years, however, there have been many threats to our freedoms.

Our **military** groups have had to fight in many, many battles to maintain the freedoms we enjoy today. Our soldiers have also fought many battles to help people in other countries. Unfortunately, when there is a war or conflict, people are injured and killed. Many of the Americans who have died in these battles are buried in Arlington National **Cemetery**.

This is the grave of Audie Murphy. He received the most honors of any World War II hero.

A Place for Heroes

★ ★ ★

Arlington National Cemetery is the most important burial ground in the country. At least one person from each American war or conflict is buried there.

The land on which the cemetery is located is in Arlington, Virginia. It is just across the Potomac River from Washington, D.C., the nation's **capital**. Thousands of Americans are buried in the cemetery, and all of them have served our country in a special way. Most of them are soldiers who were killed in battle. Some were soldiers who served in a war and died years later. Still others are important citizens, such as presidents, who served the country during their lives. In a few cases, other family members are buried there.

There are people from every state buried in Arlington National Cemetery.

A Battle Over the Land

★ ★ ★

The first battle that had an impact on Arlington National Cemetery was a battle over the land itself. A man named Robert Howsing was the first person to own the land. He was given 6,000 acres by the governor of Virginia in 1669. Eventually, the land was purchased by John Parke Custis. His family built a home there called Arlington House. The house was later occupied by Mary Custis and her husband, Colonel Robert E. Lee.

During the Civil War, Colonel Lee was a leader in the Confederate Army, which fought for the South. The property was in the northern Union's territory, however, so the Lee family was forced to leave.

This photo shows Union soldiers at Arlington House during the Civil War.

This memorial was set up for the Confederate dead buried in Arlington.

In 1864, Private William Christman became the first person to be buried on the site. Later that year, more burials took place after it was declared an official military cemetery. The bodies of many soldiers who died in the Civil War could never be identified. They were called **Unknown Soldiers**. More than 2,000 unknowns from the Civil War were buried near Arlington House in a memorial in 1866.

In 1882, the Supreme Court ruled the Lee family was still the rightful owner of the property. But with so many graves already located on the property, the Lee family didn't want the land anymore. They sold it to the United States government for $150,000. The government quickly took control of large amounts of land next to the cemetery, making it larger.

Bringing Our Soldiers Home

★ ★ ★

Burial of soldiers who died in conflicts with other countries began in 1892. In 1899, soldiers who died in the Spanish-American War became the first to be brought back to America for burial in Arlington National Cemetery. A memorial for the Spanish-American War was created in 1902.

Because Arlington National Cemetery honors the **patriots** who served our country, it is a very special place. It also attracts many visitors who want to honor the patriots buried there. Large crowds come to Arlington on special American holidays such as **Memorial Day** and the Fourth of July. In fact, a Memorial Amphitheater was built because of the large crowds that visit each Memorial Day.

An overhead view shows the amphitheater and the graves behind it.

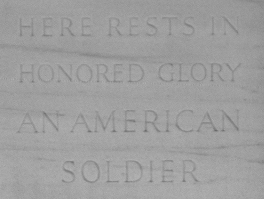

The large tomb reads "Here rests in honored glory
an American soldier known but to God."

Unknown But
Not Forgotten

★ ★ ★

One of the most special areas at Arlington National Cemetery is the Tomb of the Unknown Soldier. Originally, this tomb held the body of an Unknown Soldier from World War I. This Unknown Soldier was laid to rest there in front of the Memorial Amphitheater on **Armistice Day**, November 11, 1921.

In 1937, the tomb was placed under 24-hour guard. Even today, an armed guard watches over the tomb all day and all night. Three additional unknowns were buried in the tomb in the years since. One was from World War II, one was from the Korean War, and one was from the Vietnam War.

Special Memorials

★ ★ ★

There are several other memorials on the grounds of Arlington National Cemetery. Besides the Tomb of the Unknown Soldier and the Memorial Amphitheater, there is the Tomb of the Unknown Dead of the Civil War. You can also see the Confederate Monument and the mast of the battleship USS *Maine*. There is also a monument to those who died when the space shuttle *Challenger* exploded in 1986.

Another special memorial is the one for President John F. Kennedy. He was **assassinated** in 1963, and his body was laid to rest in a special memorial near Arlington House. As part of the memorial, an "eternal flame" was lit, which burns 24 hours a day, seven days a week.

The members of the Challenger *crew have their faces carved on the memorial.*

IN GRATEFUL
AND LOVING TRIBUTE
TO THE BRAVE CREW
OF THE UNITED STATES
SPACE SHUTTLE CHALLENGER
28 JANUARY 1986

This soldier is helping put flags on all of the gravestones on Memorial Day.

Memorial Day

★ ★ ★

Memorial Day is a special day at Arlington National Cemetery. Memorial Day was declared a national holiday in 1888. On this day we remember the people who have died while serving our country. Because Arlington National Cemetery holds the gravesites of many of these people, special ceremonies are held there every Memorial Day.

The Old Guard—the troops that help guard the Tomb of the Unknown Soldier—places a small flag on every grave in the cemetery before dawn each Memorial Day. The flags remain on the gravesites until after the Memorial Day service ends.

The Cemetery Today

★ ★ ★

There are many people who have served our country in wars and battles around the world. Many of these people are still alive today. About 15 people are buried in Arlington National Cemetery each day. It is expected that the cemetery will be full by the year 2020. At that time, more than 250,000 people will have been buried there.

Many tourists visit Arlington National Cemetery each day. They tour the grounds, visit the monuments and memorials, and remember the many people who have helped to make America the great country it is today.

Arlington National Cemetery is a peaceful place.

Glossary

Armistice Day (AR–mih–stiss DAY) The holiday that marks the end of World War I is Armistice Day. The Unknown Soldier from World War I was buried at Arlington National Cemetery on Armistice Day in 1921.

assassinated (uh–SASS–ih–nay–ted) When an important person is killed by another person, we say he or she was assassinated. President John F. Kennedy and his brother Robert F. Kennedy were assassinated. They are buried in Arlington National Cemetery.

capital (KA–pih–tull) The city in which the government offices are located is the capital. Arlington National Cemetery is located across the Potomac River from our nation's capital, Washington, D.C.

cemetery (SEH–meh–tayr–ee) A plot of land in which people are buried is called a cemetery. Arlington National Cemetery is the most famous cemetery in the United States.

Memorial Day (meh–MOR–ee–yull DAY) Memorial Day is a holiday in which we remember those who died while serving America. Memorial Day is a special day at Arlington National Cemetery.

military (MIL–ih–tar–ee) The military is the group of soldiers who fight to protect a country. Thousands of military soldiers are buried at Arlington National Cemetery.

patriots (PAY–tree–uts) A person who loves his or her country and works to protect or support it is a patriot. People who serve America are considered patriots.

Unknown Soldiers (UN–nohn SOHL–jerz) Soldiers who died in battle but could not be identified are called Unknown Soldiers. Arlington National Cemetery has several memorials that honor Unknown Soldiers.

Find Out More

IN THE LIBRARY

Jennifer Burrows. *Arlington National Cemetery*. Vero Beach, FL: Rourke, 2010.

Demarest, Chris. *Arlington: The Story of Our Nation's Cemetery*. New York: Rb Flash Point, 2010.

Schaefer, Ted and Lola M. Schaefer. *Arlington National Cemetery*. Chicago: Heinemann Library, 2006.

Stein, R. Conrad. *Arlington National Cemetery*. Chicago: Childrens Press, 1995.

ON THE WEB

Visit our Web site for lots of links about Arlington National Cemetery:
www.childsworld.com/links

Note to Parents, Teachers, and Librarians: We routinely check our Web links to make sure they're safe, active sites—so encourage your readers to check them out!

Index